This book belongs to

_____

Given on the day of their Baptism:

_____

Which took place at:

_____

Here I am at my Baptism

Jesus Speaks to Me About
MY BAPTISM

BY ANGELA M. BURRIN

ILLUSTRATED BY MARIA CRISTINA LO CASCIO

I Know My Sheep!

"I AM THE GOOD SHEPHERD. I KNOW MY SHEEP AND MY SHEEP KNOW ME."
JOHN 10:14

I am Jesus, and I want to tell you about that very special day when you received the Sacrament of Baptism. If you were baptized as a baby, you won't remember it. But that doesn't matter, because I do! And in this book, I'll explain everything that happened.

I was so happy the day your parents brought you to the church to be baptized. Do you know why? Because it was the beginning of our special friendship! On that day, you became a child of your heavenly Father. You also became a member of a special family—the Catholic Church.

I am the Good Shepherd of that family, and you are one of my sheep! Just as a shepherd takes care of his sheep, I want to take care of you all of your life.

Let me tell you about the job of a shepherd. He makes sure his sheep have good grass to eat. He always stays with them and protects them from wild animals. If a sheep wanders off, he searches for it until he finds it. And did you know that sheep always recognize the voice of their shepherd?

Just as sheep recognize the voice of their shepherd, everyone who is baptized can hear my voice. Remember—I am your Good Shepherd, and I am always with you!

SO TURN THE PAGE, AND READ MORE ABOUT THE DAY YOU WERE BAPTIZED!

What Name Do You Give This Child?

"You shall name him Jesus, for he will save his people from their sins."
Matthew 1:21

If you were baptized as a baby, you were probably wearing a special white gown. Your parents, godparents, family, and friends arrived at the church with you. Ask your parents if you were quiet or crying!

The priest welcomed everyone—including you! He said you were a gift to your parents from God. He reminded everyone that your heavenly Father now wanted to give you his own life through the Sacrament of Baptism. Isn't that awesome?

Next, the priest asked your parents, "What name do you give your child?"

Your name is very important. Mine is special too. Do you know how I got it? Over two thousand years ago, your heavenly Father sent the angel Gabriel to a young girl in Nazareth called Mary. She was afraid, but the angel said to her, "Do not be afraid. You are going to have a baby, and you are to name him Jesus." My name means "God saves his people."

Write your baptismal name on this line:

....

Ask your parents why they chose that name for you.

Your Parents and Godparents

"EVERY YEAR HIS PARENTS WENT TO JERUSALEM FOR THE FEAST OF THE PASSOVER."
LUKE 2:41

This is what happened next. The priest asked your mom and dad, "What do you ask of God's Church for your child?" They replied, "Baptism."

But since you were still a baby, your parents had to promise that they would teach you all about the Catholic faith. They promised to teach you to love God, your family, and your friends, and to make choices that are pleasing to God. Your godparents promised to help your parents teach you.

My parents, Mary and Joseph, taught me that my Father in heaven loved me. We read the Scriptures together and they showed me how to pray. You can pray too—on your way to school or when you play with your friends. Pray

anywhere or at any time, and your Father will listen to you. And you can talk to me after you receive me in Holy Communion.

And just as your parents take you to church, my parents took me to the Temple in Jerusalem. We went every year to celebrate the feast of Passover. I remember the long walk from Nazareth. It was fun because our relatives, friends, and neighbors walked with us. Passover was a very special feast when we remembered the night that Moses led our people out of slavery in Egypt.

ON THIS LINE, WRITE THE NAMES OF YOUR GODPARENTS:

....

ASK YOUR PARENTS WHY THEY CHOSE THEM. HAVE YOU EVER THANKED YOUR PARENTS
AND GODPARENTS FOR TEACHING YOU ABOUT THE CATHOLIC FAITH?

Your "New Life" Birthday

"No one can see the kingdom of God unless he is born again."
John 3:3

When you make the Sign of the Cross, you pray to the Trinity—Father, Son, and Holy Spirit. At your baptism, the priest made the Sign of the Cross on your forehead and asked your parents and godparents to do the same. Then he invited everyone to listen to a reading from the Bible. Perhaps he read about a man named Nicodemus.

Nicodemus was a leader of the Jewish people who came to me secretly in the middle of the night. "Teacher," he said to me, "I know you are from God because of all the miracles you do." I said to him, "No one can see the kingdom of God without being born from above." This puzzled him. "How can a grown person be born again?" he asked. I answered, "No one can enter the kingdom of God without being born of water and the Holy Spirit."

You were born again and received new life in the Holy Spirit in the Sacrament of Baptism. Isn't that exciting? That's why I want every person to be baptized. I want everyone to be able to enjoy life in my Father's kingdom, which is full of love, joy, and peace! Every day, please say "yes" to living the new life you received at your baptism.

Do you know the day you were baptized? That's your "new life" birthday.
You can find that date on your baptismal certificate. Ask your parents to show you.
Then write the date on this line:

....

The Saints Pray for You!

"THE GRACE OF THE LORD JESUS BE WITH ALL THE SAINTS."
REVELATION 22:21

At your baptism, the saints prayed for you! The priest said, "Holy Mary, Mother of God," and everyone responded, "Pray for us." Then he called on other saints: Saint John the Baptist, Saint Joseph, and Saints Peter and Paul. He even prayed to the saint you are named after!

Saints are men and women who had a special relationship with me. They came from many different countries and did many different things. In fact, there are so many saints that you could probably find one for each letter of the alphabet! How about Francis of Assisi for "F" and Therese of Lisieux for "T"?

But the saints all had one thing in common. They all received—just like you—new life in the Holy Spirit in the Sacrament of Baptism. Now they are enjoying heaven! They see me face to face. They stand before the glorious throne of your heavenly Father. Close your eyes for a moment and see this in your mind.

The earthly work of the saints is over, but they are still working here in heaven with me. Talk to your special saints. Tell them what you would like me to do for you. Perhaps you need help with your schoolwork or want to get along better with a brother or sister. Just as everyone did at your baptism, ask the saints right now to pray for you!

HERE IS SAINT JOSEPH IN HIS WORKSHOP WITH JESUS.
WHO IS YOUR FAVORITE SAINT? WRITE HIS OR HER NAME HERE:

....

Blessing of the Water

GOD SAID, "COME OUT OF THE ARK."
GENESIS 8:15-16

On the day of your baptism, your parents and godparents stood around a font filled with water. If you can find a photo, you will see who is holding you. The water in the font started out as just ordinary water from the faucet. But at your baptism, the priest put his right hand into the water and prayed a blessing. Through the Holy Spirit, the blessed water now had the power to wash away sin.

The story in the Bible of Noah and the ark is also about water. God saw how Noah loved him and so he told Noah to build an ark. It rained for forty days and forty nights, but Noah and his family were safe in the ark. After the rain ended, the ark came to rest on land. Noah and his family who were in the ark began a new life.

The sin that is washed away in the waters of baptism is called "original sin." Adam and Eve committed the first—or original—sin when they disobeyed God. Ever since then, every person who is born needs the waters of baptism to save them from sin and give them new life. It was because of my death on the cross and my resurrection that the waters of baptism can wash you clean. Isn't it wonderful?

WHAT IS THE NAME OF THE PRIEST OR DEACON WHO BAPTIZED YOU? WRITE IT HERE:

....

You Are Baptized!

"This is my Son, whom I love; with him I am well pleased."
Matthew 3:17

Just before you were baptized, your parents had to make an act of faith—because you were only a baby and couldn't do it yourself! They said they rejected sin and the works of Satan. They said they believed in God and the holy Catholic Church. Now that you are older, you say, "I believe" when you pray the Creed at Mass.

Then came the moment of baptism. The priest took some water from the font. "I baptize you in the name of the Father," he said, pouring water over your head, "and of the Son," he said, pouring more water, "and of the Holy Spirit," he said, pouring water a third time. And so you became a child of God!

Do you remember where I was baptized? It was in the River Jordan. My cousin John was baptizing the crowds for the forgiveness of their sins. At first, John didn't want to baptize me because he knew I was without sin. But I said it was part of my Father's plan, so John lowered me into the water. Then the Holy Spirit, in the form of a dove, hovered over me, and I heard my Father in heaven say, "You are my son. I love you. I am pleased with you."

SOME CHURCHES HAVE A LITTLE POOL THEY USE FOR BAPTISM TO IMMERSE THE BABY COMPLETELY.
ASK YOUR PARENTS HOW YOU WERE BAPTIZED!

You Are Anointed with Chrism

SAMUEL TOOK THE OIL AND ANOINTED DAVID
AND THE SPIRIT OF THE LORD CAME POWERFULLY UPON HIM.
1 SAMUEL 16:13

Do you know what chrism is? After you were baptized, you were anointed with chrism—oil made from crushed olives. It is usually scented with the oil from balsam trees, so it smells a bit like a Christmas tree.

Chrism is a sign of the power and strength of the Holy Spirit. The priest dipped his finger in the chrism and made the Sign of the Cross on your head. You immediately received heavenly power and strength!

Because you have been anointed with chrism, you can live a life set apart for me. Satan wants to tempt you to sin. When you are tempted to do what is wrong, remember that I gave you power and strength at your baptism. Pray, "Jesus, help me right now to make a good choice."

King David was someone who had heavenly power and strength. As a young man, the prophet Samuel anointed him to be the King of Israel. David was a good king. When he sinned, he asked my Father to forgive him and he changed his ways. David also played the harp, wrote psalms, and loved to dance, sing, and praise my Father. And do you remember that he killed the giant Goliath with just a single stone?

ASK YOUR PASTOR IF YOU CAN SMELL THE CHRISM OIL AT YOUR CHURCH.

Your White Garment

THEY HAVE WASHED THEIR ROBES AND MADE THEM WHITE IN THE BLOOD OF THE LAMB.
REVELATION 7:14

The amazing grace of the Sacrament of Baptism makes your soul as white as snow. That's why the priest laid a small white garment on you as a sign of purity. Then he prayed that you would keep your soul unstained so that you could have everlasting life in heaven with my Father and me.

Do you know that your Father wants you to be with him in heaven forever?

Even before the creation of the world, my Father was thinking about you. Remember, heaven is a wonderful place—a place where everyone is happy and where there is no sadness or sickness.

My apostle John had a vision of heaven when he was on the island of Patmos. He saw people dressed in white robes and singing praises to God. They had been baptized and cleansed in my precious blood, and they were wearing white robes because their souls were now pure—as white as snow.

You can keep your soul pure by choosing to avoid anything that will get you into trouble. Look for ways every day to be kind, helpful, and generous. And remember, if you do something wrong, I am waiting to forgive you in the Sacrament of Reconciliation.

ONE MORE THING: BEFORE YOU GO TO SLEEP AT NIGHT, ASK THE HOLY SPIRIT TO REMIND YOU
OF ANYTHING YOU'VE DONE WRONG THAT DAY. THEN SAY AN ACT OF CONTRITION.
HOW IT PLEASES ME TO HEAR YOUR PRAYERS!

Your Baptismal Candle

THE VIRGINS WHO WERE READY WENT IN WITH HIM TO THE WEDDING BANQUET.
MATTHEW 25:10

At your baptism, you received a candle that was lit from the large Easter candle on the altar. Do you know why? Your baptismal candle is the symbol of my light. The priest looked at you and said, "Receive the light of Christ." Then he prayed that you would always keep the flame of faith alive in your heart. He also prayed that you would be ready to meet me when I come again.

Here's a story I once told the crowds about being ready for my Second Coming. There were ten young women who were invited to a wedding banquet. Five of them took extra oil for their lanterns. They were the wise ones. The other five couldn't be bothered. They were the foolish ones. All the young women fell asleep waiting for the bridegroom to come, and their lanterns burned up a lot of oil. When the bridegroom came, only the wise ones had enough oil left to go with the bridegroom into the banquet. The foolish ones ran off to get more oil. But when they returned, the door was closed.

No one but my Father knows when my Second Coming will be. But when it happens, I want everyone to be ready to run out and meet me!

DO YOU HAVE A BIBLE? READ THE STORY OF THE YOUNG WOMEN WAITING FOR THE BRIDEGROOM IN MATTHEW 25:1-13.

Your Mouth and Ears Are Opened!

"HE MAKES EVEN THE DEAF HEAR AND THE MUTE SPEAK."
MARK 7:37

There was still something for the priest to do at your baptism. He touched your ears and mouth with his thumb and prayed, "The Lord Jesus made the deaf hear and the dumb speak. May he soon touch your ears to receive his word, and your mouth to proclaim his faith."

One day some people brought a man to me who was deaf and who could hardly talk. They begged me to heal him. I took the man away from the crowd and put my fingers into his ears. Then I spat on my fingers and put them on the man's tongue. I said, "Ephphatha!" which means, "Be opened!" The man was amazed! He could hear and speak clearly.

What do you think was the first thing the healed man said to his friends? Perhaps he said, "Jesus loves me! Look what he's done for me!" Just like this man, talk about me and what I have done for you with your friends and family.

Remember when I told you that everyone who is baptized can hear my voice? Ask the Holy Spirit to give you "spiritual ears" so that you can listen carefully when you're at Mass and hear what I want to tell you.

HERE'S ANOTHER THING YOU CAN DO.
FIND A SPECIAL PLACE IN YOUR HOME—A PRAYER CORNER—WHERE YOU AND I CAN SPEAK AND
LISTEN TO EACH OTHER!

Give My Love to Others

"Let the children come to me."
Matthew 19:14

The Our Father is a special prayer that I taught my disciples. Everyone prayed that prayer together at your baptism. Even though you couldn't say the words yet, you were now my Father's special child, and so everyone was praying the words for you.

Then the priest prayed a blessing over your mother and father. How happy they were that you had become a child of God! Ask your parents what happened after they took you home from church. Maybe there was a party and some cake!

Children are very special to me. One day my disciples tried to stop the children from coming to me for a blessing. But I said to them, "Let the children come to me."

And I'm still saying that to parents today whenever babies are born—"Let the children come to me." That's why I'm so happy that you have received the Sacrament of Baptism. That was the first way you came to me. I want adults, too, who haven't been baptized to receive the sacrament. And if you haven't received your first Holy Communion or Confirmation yet, start looking forward to the time when you will receive these sacraments!

What is next for you? Try to show others by your good example how to live the new life you received at your baptism. Give my love to others, and tell them about the special relationship you and I have.

And remember—I am always with you! And I love you!

PRAY AN OUR FATHER FOR ALL CHILDREN ABOUT TO BE BAPTIZED.

Prayer of Thanksgiving for My Baptism

I thank you, Jesus, that . . .

Our special friendship began when I was baptized.

My heavenly Father loves me and calls me his beloved child.

The Holy Spirit lives in me and I now have new life.

I praise you, Jesus, that . . .

Original sin was washed away in the waters of Baptism.

I am a member of the Catholic Church.

My parents and godparents are teaching me about the Catholic faith.

I love you, Jesus.

You are my Good Shepherd
You died on the cross for my sins
Every day I want to make choices that please you.

I trust you, Jesus.

I give you my heart.
You are alive and always with me.
You will never stop loving me!
Amen.

The Apostles' Creed

I believe in God, the Father almighty,
creator of heaven and earth.
I believe in Jesus Christ, his only Son, our Lord.
He was conceived by the power of the Holy Spirit
and born of the Virgin Mary.
He suffered under Pontius Pilate,
was crucified, died, and was buried.
He descended to the dead.
On the third day he rose again.
He ascended into heaven,
and is seated at the right hand
of the Father.
He will come again to judge the living
and the dead.

I believe in the Holy Spirit,
the holy catholic Church,
the communion of saints,
the forgiveness of sins,
the resurrection of the body,
and the life everlasting. Amen.

Act of Contrition

My God, I am sorry for my sins with all my heart.
In choosing to do wrong and failing to do good,
I have sinned against you whom I should love above all things.
I firmly intend with your help, to do penance, to sin no more,
and to avoid whatever leads me to sin. Amen.

The Our Father

Our Father, who art in heaven,
hallowed be thy name;
thy kingdom come;
thy will be done on earth
as it is in heaven.
Give us this day our daily bread;
and forgive us our trespasses
as we forgive those who trespass against us;
and lead us not into temptation
but deliver us from evil. Amen.

The Hail Mary

Hail Mary, full of grace, the Lord is with you.
Blessed are you among women,
and blessed is the fruit of your womb, Jesus.
Holy Mary, Mother of God, pray for us sinners,
now and at the hour of our death.
Amen.

The Sign of the Cross

In the name of the Father, and of the Son,
and of the Holy Spirit. Amen.

WHITE GARMENT
(baptismal gown)

BAPTISMAL FONT

BAPTISMAL CANDLE

EASTER CANDLE

CHRISM OIL

CRUCIFIX

LECTIONARY

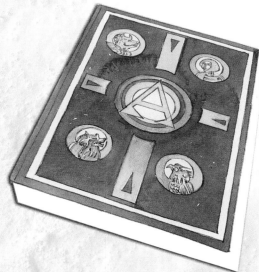

These people came to my Baptism